J 546787
387.7 12.95
Amo
Amos
Let's go to the airport

DATE DUE			
NO 12 '94			

GREAT RIVER REGIONAL LIBRARY

St. Cloud, Minnesota 56301

AIRPORT

Library Edition Published 1990

© Cherrytree Press Ltd 1989
© Marshall Cavendish Limited 1990

Library Edition produced by DPM Services Limited

All rights reserved. No part of this book may be reproduced or utilized in any form or by any means electronic or mechanical including photocopying, recording, or by any information storage and retrieval system, without permission from the copyright holders.

Printed in Italy

Library of Congress Cataloging-in-Publication Data

Graham, Alison.
  Airport / by Alison Graham
    p. cm. – (Lets go to)
  Includes index.
  Summary: Examines the different parts of an airport and describes the various operations and activities.
  ISBN 1-85435-239-3
    1. Airports – Juvenile literature. [1. Airports.] I. Title. II. Series: Graham, Alison. Lets go to.
  TL725.G69 1990
  387.7'36 – dc20   89-17335
                                                                                 CIP
                                                                                  AC

Let's Go To
THE AIRPORT

By Janine Amos
Illustrated by Peter Lowe

546787

MARSHALL CAVENDISH
New York · London · Toronto · Sydney

624726

planes

terminal

buses

runway

Every day people fly on airplanes. Some of them are going on their vacations. Some of them are making business trips. Wherever they are going, their journey starts and ends at an airport.

Let's go and see what happens at an airport.

We arrive at the terminal building. It is very busy. There are lots of buses and taxis there. People are carrying suitcases or pushing carts.

airport manager

Inside the terminal, we meet the airport manager. He is in charge of all the people who work at the airport. He has to make sure that everything runs smoothly.

Planes fly all over the world from this airport. One plane takes off every four minutes.

The manager shows us a plan of the airport. He points out the terminal building.

Near the terminal there is a huge parking lot. People leave their cars there while they are away.

Behind the terminal, there are two runways. Planes take off from them and land on them. A tall control tower in the middle controls all the planes. Nearby, there are huge sheds called hangars. The planes are kept in them when they are not flying.

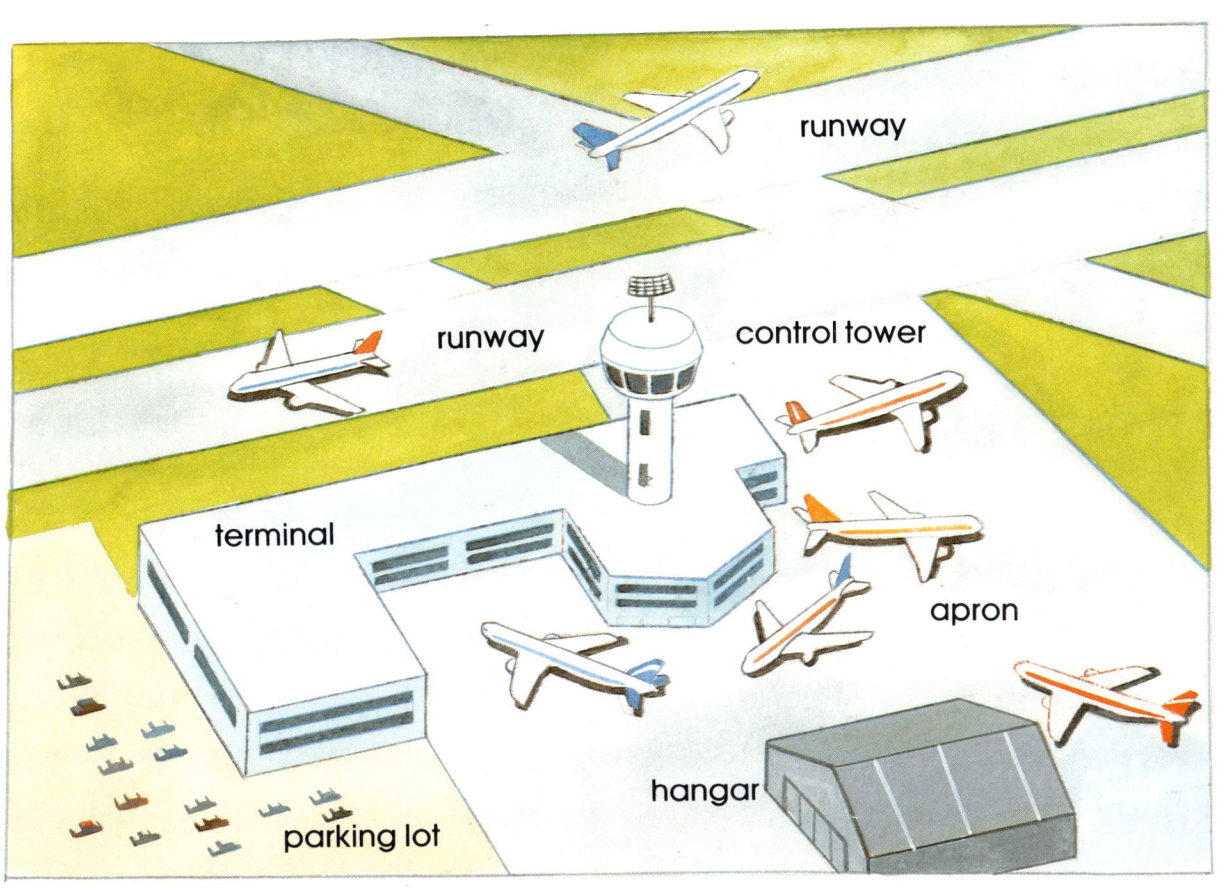

monitor

luggage cart

We look around the terminal. It is noisy and exciting. People have carts piled high with luggage. They ask questions at the information desk. They look at the times of flights on display monitors. They all seem to be in a hurry.

The terminal is like a small town. There are stores and restaurants, mailboxes, telephones and a bank. Some people are going to other countries. They need to change their money.

Many people are standing in line. They are passengers waiting to check in. They give their tickets to the ticket agent at the check-in desk. The agent weighs their luggage and labels it. Then it goes on a moving belt to be loaded onto the plane. The agent gives each passenger a boarding card. This allows them onto their plane.

departure lounge

The passengers often have to wait until their plane is ready. They may go to the store and buy a book to read on the plane. They may have a cup of coffee in the restaurant. Whatever they do, they keep an eye on the monitors. When their flight is displayed, they have to be ready to board. They also listen for announcements from loudspeakers.

observation deck

If there is time, people can go outside and watch the planes. There is a special observation deck. It has a good view of the runway.

You can see the planes in their parking places. These are called stands. One plane is on the runway. It goes faster and faster and faster. Then it takes off. You can see its wheels.

walkway

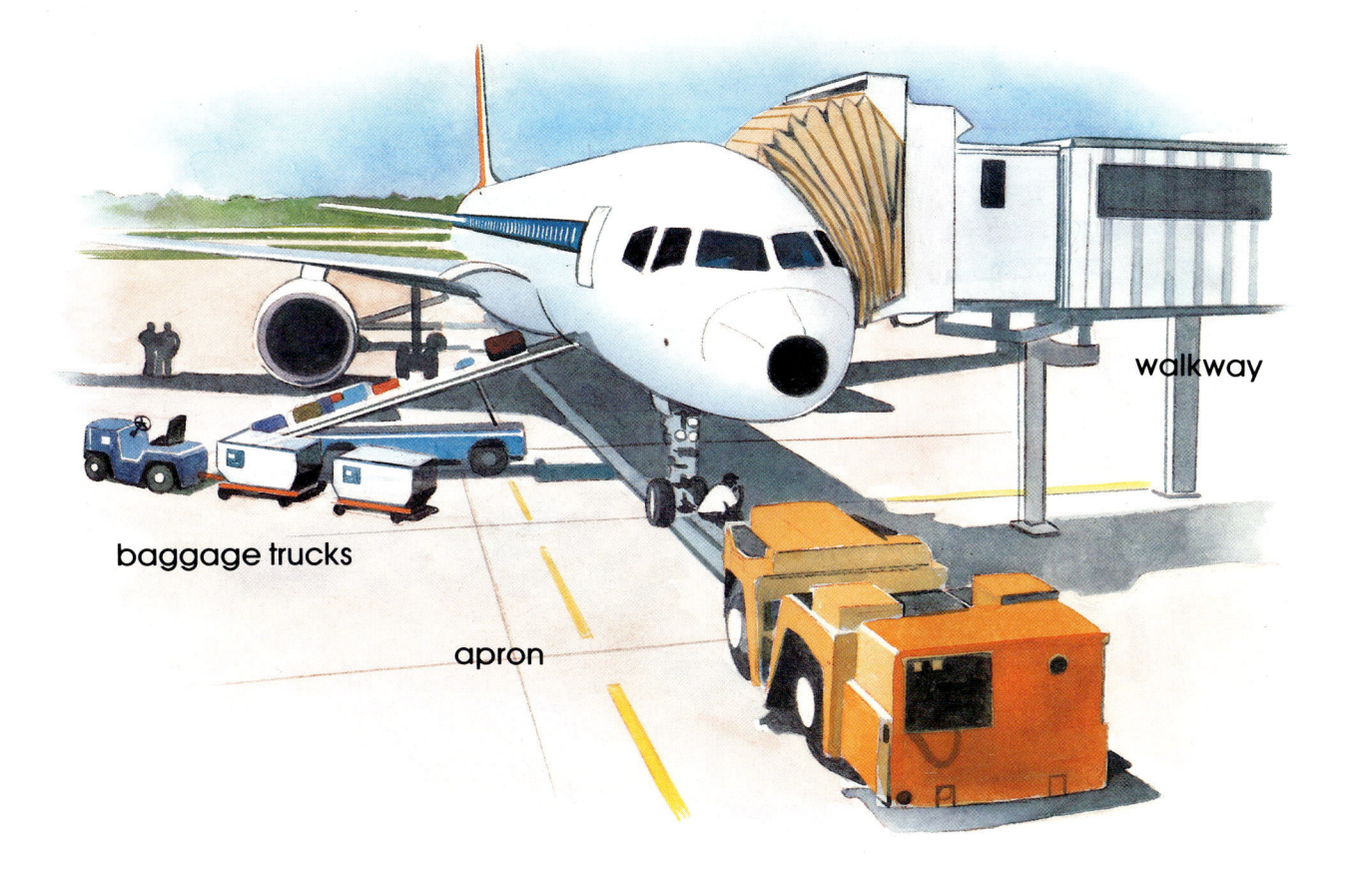

baggage trucks

apron

Another plane has just landed. It goes slowly right up to the terminal. A covered walkway comes out to meet the plane. The passengers walk through it.

The baggage comes down a ramp. Trucks take it to the terminal. Cleaners go on board to get the plane ready for its next flight. Engineers check every part of the plane.

loaders

fuel pipe

apron

The area where the plane waits is called the apron. The plane cannot leave until any repairs have been made.

The passengers' baggage is loaded into the hold. There may be mail and other cargo as well.

Food for the passengers' meals is loaded into the cabin. The meals are in sealed containers.

The plane takes on fuel from a pipe. The fuel is stored in big tanks under the ground.

Inside the airport, the plane's crew is getting ready. The captain has a flight plan. It tells him where the plane is going. It gives details of the route. It also tells him how fast to fly.

The captain picks up a weather report. If bad weather is expected, he may not be able to land. He may need extra fuel to fly on to another airport.

The captain goes through the plan with his crew. He points out any problems for them to watch for. Then the flight crew boards the plane.

The crew makes the pre-flight checks. Everything must work perfectly. There are many controls on the flight deck. The plane cannot leave the ground if there is anything wrong.

security gate

Before the people get on the plane, they have to be checked, too. This is the work of the security staff. They search people and luggage for weapons or bombs.

The passengers walk through a special gate. If they are carrying anything made of metal, an alarm sounds. Passengers' passports may also be looked at.

The staff checks all the hand luggage. People put their handbags or briefcases onto a moving belt. This takes the bags through a scanning machine. The machine X-rays the bags. The person checking the bags can see on a screen the shape of what is inside them.

After they have been checked, the passengers go to the gate. The plane is waiting for them.

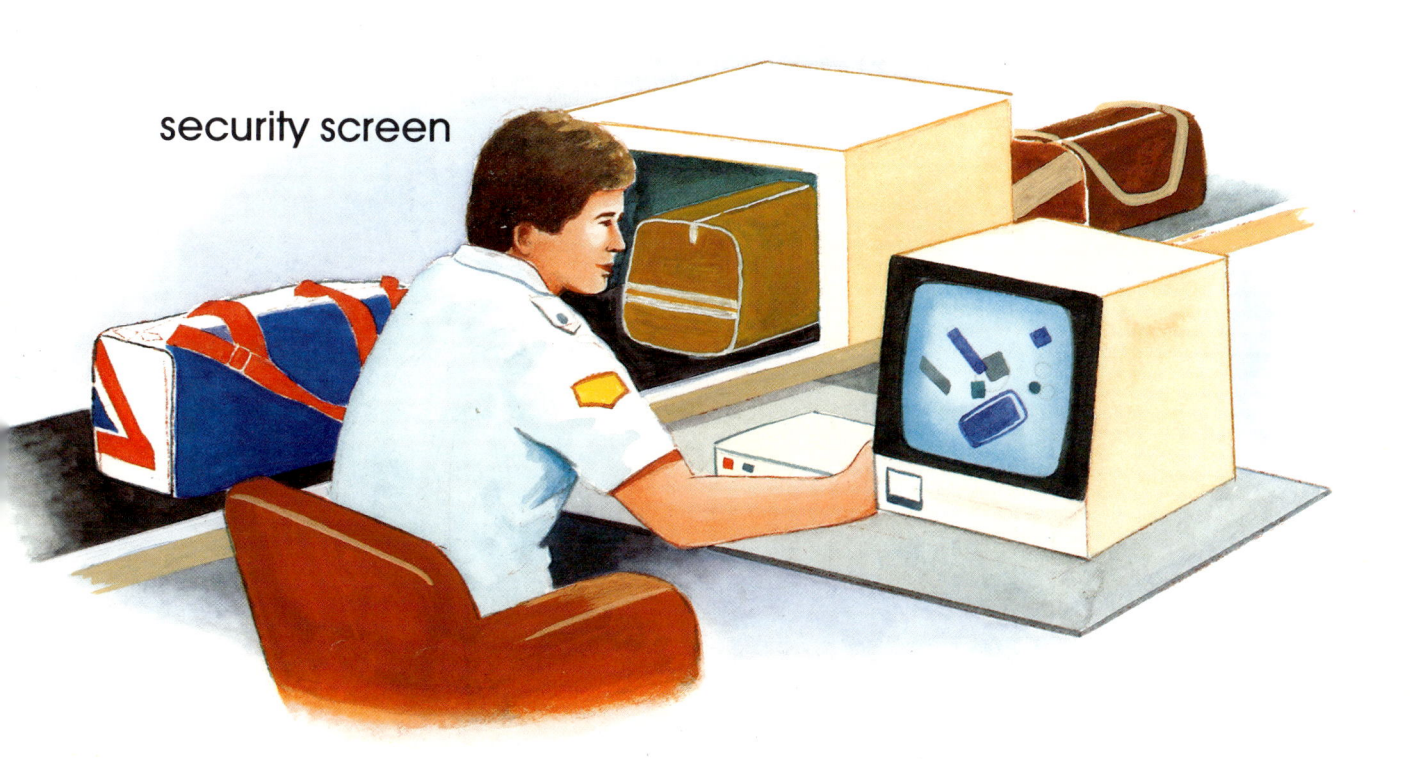

security screen

control tower

The passengers board the plane. The captain and his co-pilot talk to the control tower. The air traffic controllers tell them which runway they can use.

The plane taxis to the runway. Then it waits for its turn to take off.

The air traffic controllers are in contact with all the planes. Some are landing. Some are taking off. Others are waiting for permission to land or take off.

The controllers guide each plane. They can see in all directions from the tower. They also have a huge panel of instruments. They can see planes in the air on their radar screens. Each one shows up as a "blip" of light.

air traffic controllers

instrument panel

emergency services

Take-off and landing are the most dangerous parts of each flight. The control tower keeps in touch with the emergency services. Fire engines and ambulances are ready in case anything goes wrong.

The runways are lined with lights. They help pilots land safely at night and when it is foggy.

runway

baggage carousel

When a plane lands, the passengers walk to the terminal. Trucks bring their luggage to the baggage claim area. The luggage arrives in the baggage area on a moving belt. The belt goes round and round, so that all the people can pick up their luggage. It is called a carousel.

There are carts for people to put heavy bags on.

customs official

Everyone who has been out of the country has to go through customs. You are not allowed to bring some things into the country. You have to pay tax on some other things.

Customs officials make sure you do not smuggle things in. They may search your case. They may search you.

container

It is not only people who fly from airports. Planes carry freight as well. Some planes only carry freight cargo. The goods they carry are stored in large hangars.

Loading the planes is a difficult job. The cargo must not be too heavy. Its weight must be spread out evenly in the cargo hold.

cargo plane

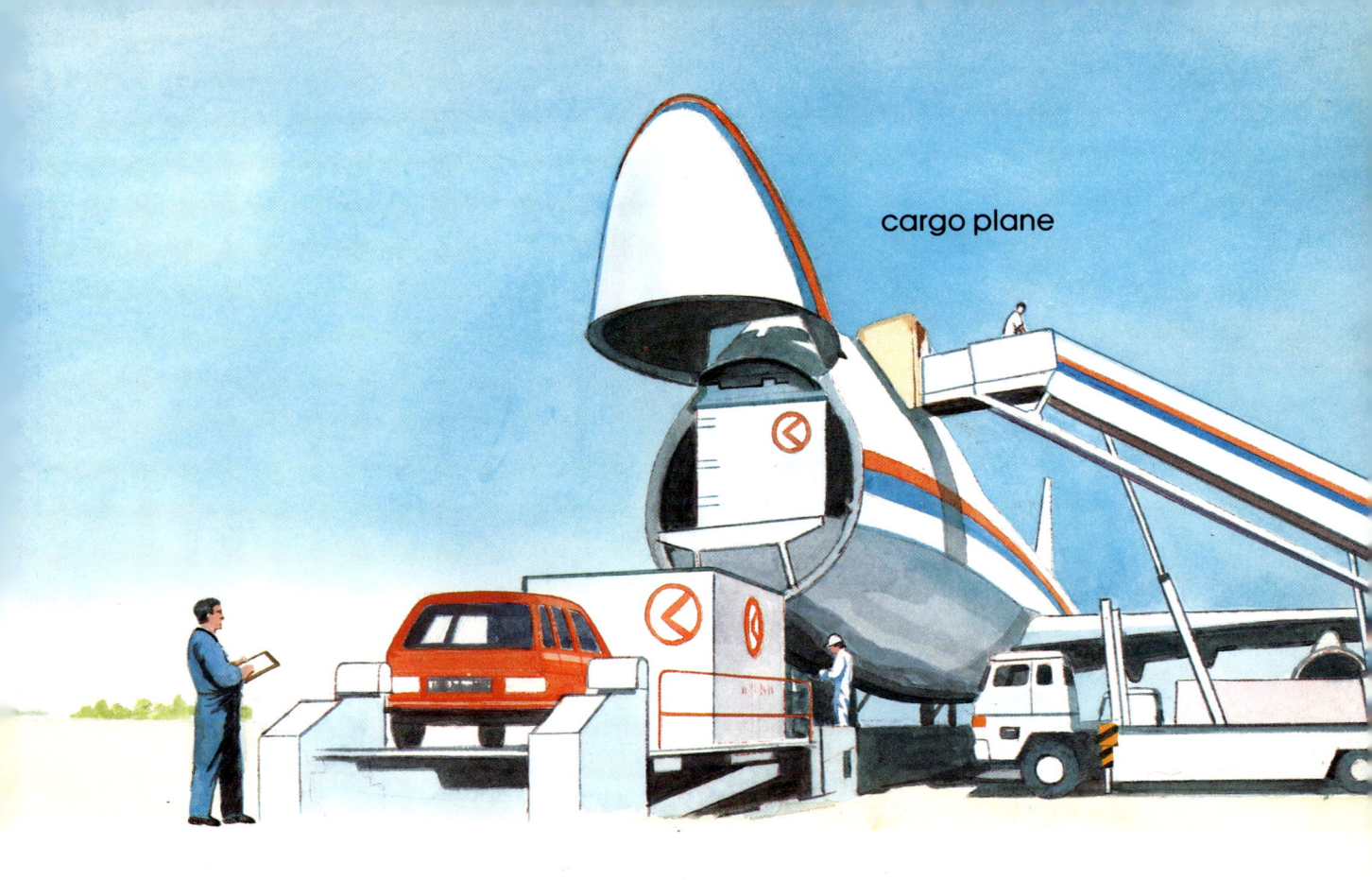

Most freight is packed into large metal boxes called containers. Some are the size of a truck. Special platforms lift them up into the hold.

It is expensive to send freight by plane. So usually people only send things that cannot travel slowly. Fruit and flowers spoil quickly. So they are often sent by plane.

maintenance men

maintenance hangar

wheels

We watch the ground crew working in the hangar. Once everything is all right, the planes can fly again. One plane is ready. They wheel it outside.

Now that we have seen everything at the airport, we can go home. The airport manager gives us each a Fact File which answers our questions. Then he gives us a surprise. We are going up in the plane. Now we shall see the airport from the sky.

engineer   engine

Planes do not fly all the time. After each plane has flown a certain number of hours it is examined. This is like a doctor's examination. Skilled engineers look at every moving part. They check the controls and all the electrical systems.

They X-ray the body and wings to make sure that there are no tiny cracks. If any part is even slightly worn or broken, they replace it.

Fact File

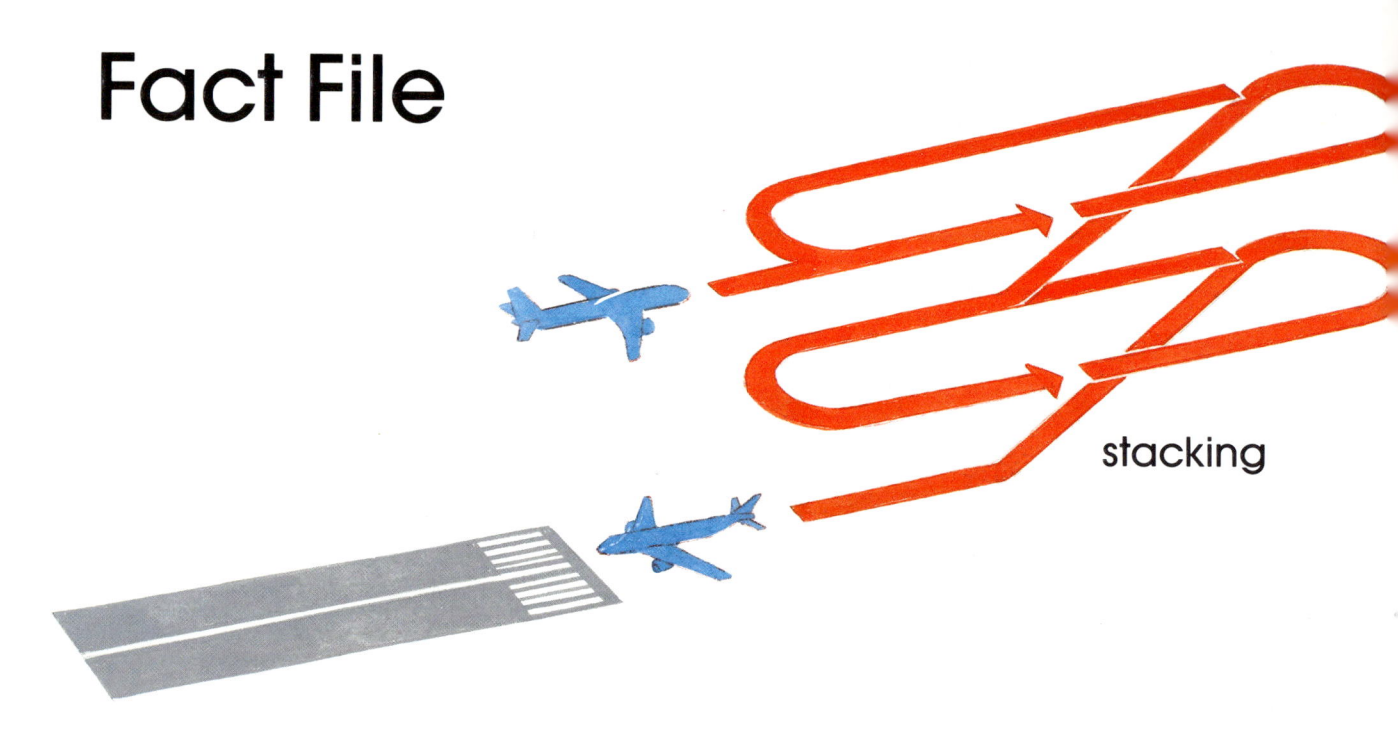

stacking

What are the main parts of an airport?
There are four main parts of an airport. They are the **terminal**, the **control tower**, the **runways** and the **hangars**.

How do planes know when it is safe to take off?
The control tower tells the pilot. The controllers can see the runways. They can see all the planes for miles around on their radar screens. They know when there is a runway free. They know when the plane's route is clear.

How do planes know when to land?
As planes approach the airport, they ask if they can land. Often, they have to wait. The control tower tells them to circle. The planes circle one above the other. This is called stacking. When there is room for a plane to

land, the control tower tells the plane at the bottom of the stack to land.

What happens to the planes between airports?

There are radar ground stations all along a plane's route. The stations send out strong signals which track the planes. Signals from these stations tell the airport where the plane is. This way, air traffic controllers make sure that the planes keep a safe distance apart. Planes traveling in opposite directions fly at different heights. This means there is no danger of them crashing into each other.

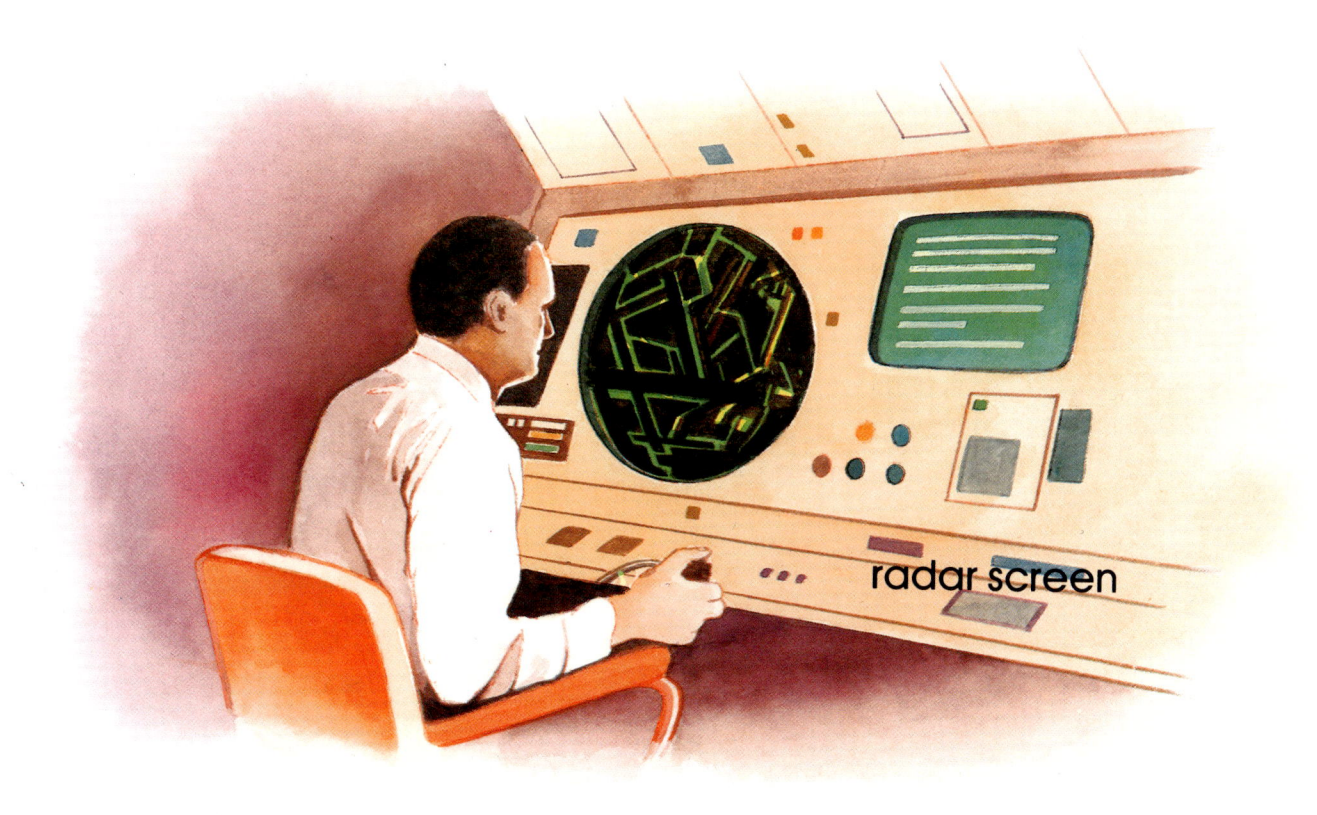

radar screen

Index

airplanes (planes) 4-7,
 10-13, 15-21, 24, 26-31
airport manager 6, 29
air traffic controllers 20, 21,
 30
apron 7, 13-15

baggage 13, 15
baggage carousel 24
baggage hall 24
baggage trucks 13
bank 9
boarding card 10
bombs 18
book 11
buses 4, 5

cabin 15
captain 16, 17, 20
cargo 15, 26, 27
cargo plane 27
carts 5, 8, 24
check-in 10
checking
 luggage 19
 passengers 18
 passports 18
 planes 13, 28
 pre-flight 17
 tickets 10
cleaners 13
containers 27
control tower 7, 20-22, 30,
 31

co-pilot 20
crew 16, 17
customs 25

departure lounge 11
display screen 8, 9, 11

emergency services 22
engineers 13, 28, 29
engines 28, 29

fire engines 22
flight deck 17
flight plan 16, 17
food 15
fuel 15, 16
fuel pipe 14

gate 15, 19
goods hangar 26
ground station 31
guns 18

hand luggage 19
hangars 7, 26, 28-30
hold 15, 26

information desk 9

landing 21, 22
loaders 14
loading 15, 26, 27
loudspeakers 11
luggage 10, 18
luggage cart 8, 24

mail 15

mailboxes 9
maintenance hangar 28
money 9

observation deck 12

parking lot 7
passengers 10, 13, 15, 18,
 20
passports 18
pilots 22
planes (airplanes) 4-7,
 10-13, 15-21, 24, 26-29
pre-flight checks 17

radar screens 21, 31
restaurants 9, 11
runway 7, 12, 20, 22, 30

scanning machine 19
screens 9, 11
security 18, 19
stacking 30
stands 12
stores 9, 11
suitcases 5

take-off 12, 21, 22
taxis 5
telephones 9
terminal 4-7, 9, 13, 30

weather report 16